Locker Room Talk

Of Mice, Men and a Bunch of Other Creatures

Locker Room Talk

Written and Illustrated by Oshri Hakak

BUTTERFLYON BOOKS

First Edition
Copyright © 2020, by Oshri Hakak
All Rights Reserved

Locker Room Talk
Written and Illustrated by Oshri Hakak

Published by Butterflyon Books
Los Angeles
ISBN 978-1-7349790-2-2

For all my brothers.

If you put your ear up close against the door of the guys' locker room, so you can hear every little peep, you can hear a lot going on...

"Dog, I love sharing this vulnerable heart-space together with you after practice."

"Dog, you took the words out of my mouth and I am so good with that."

"Bro, did you see her?"

"Yes. Totally opened-up my heart. What a kind and creative person. I'm looking forward to having a beautiful platonic relationship with her, guided by clear and respectful boundaries."

"That's what I'm talkin' about."

"Bro, I wonder what this world would be like if the definition of a superhero wasn't just a person who's good at tearing someone else to shreds?"

"Bro... your question tickles me delightfully. I think the core superpower of all us men is kindness and integrity."

"Nice win we had!"

"The real win will be when we change the rules so that the better anyone does, the better it is for everyone. Then a victory for anyone won't force anyone else to hide in their shell."

"So true."

"You know something? We're all really wonderful."

"Dude, thank you. I'm so done with being divisive and destructively competitive with one another. I'm all about being kind and responsible for all my words and actions now, for the benefit of the greatest good. Constantly expanding my sense of what that even means!"

"I see you leveling up. Mad props."

"Bro... Bro... You are SUCH a chicken! How'd you get to be so comfortable being your authentic self?"

"I wouldn't say I'm always exactly comfortable with it, I just prefer it to not being genuine."

"Wow... so brave and vulnerable. Yep, I guess when it comes to being true to ourselves there's really just no one else to pass the
buck buck buck to."

"Exactly."

"Hey... I got a problem with you... You're being all self-critical, and so ungentle with yourself! Not hip... not hip at all, my Brother."

"Bro, you are really on point and I appreciate you calling me out on that."

"I just want to see you succeed and be happy. I care about you."

"I care about you, too."

"Listen up, Bro, we've got to stop treating anyone or anything like objects. Even objects."

"I totally hear you, my sweet friend. One big hop of consciousness."

"Hey, thanks for your patience and support, Bro."

"Brother, what kind of society would I be cultivating for future generations if I didn't do my best to be patient, supportive, kind and sensitive? It's my impatience, meanness and selfishness I'm shedding."

"You win. Let's hug it out."

"My heart is roaring with gratitude for you."

"We really are a magical team."

"What if bro-hugs were never labeled as gay, and beyond that what if being gay wasn't stigmatized?"

"That would be super chill... I think we'd be hugging a lot more often and I would probably feel a lot more secure with who I am as a male in this world... You DTH?"

"You know it, Brother. I'm always Down To Hug."

"Bro... I made a big mistake..."

"Awesome, Bro— sounds like a wonderful learning opportunity. Fantastic."

"Aw... Thank you... You're always spouting such beautiful forgiveness."

"Well, you know the biggest mistake— and the one we can choose to fix in any moment— is not forgiving."

"True."

"You know, your gentle, steady and loving presence really provides me with the purrfect sanctuary for healing deep emotional scars. It's just so... meowesome..."

"It's a privilege to be here fur you, Brother."

"You think you can man-up?"

"Well, I did plant a tree with one of my ants the other day."

"Wow— that puts you a step ahead of me!"

"No such thing Brother- how about we plant something together tomorrow?"

"Let's do it!"

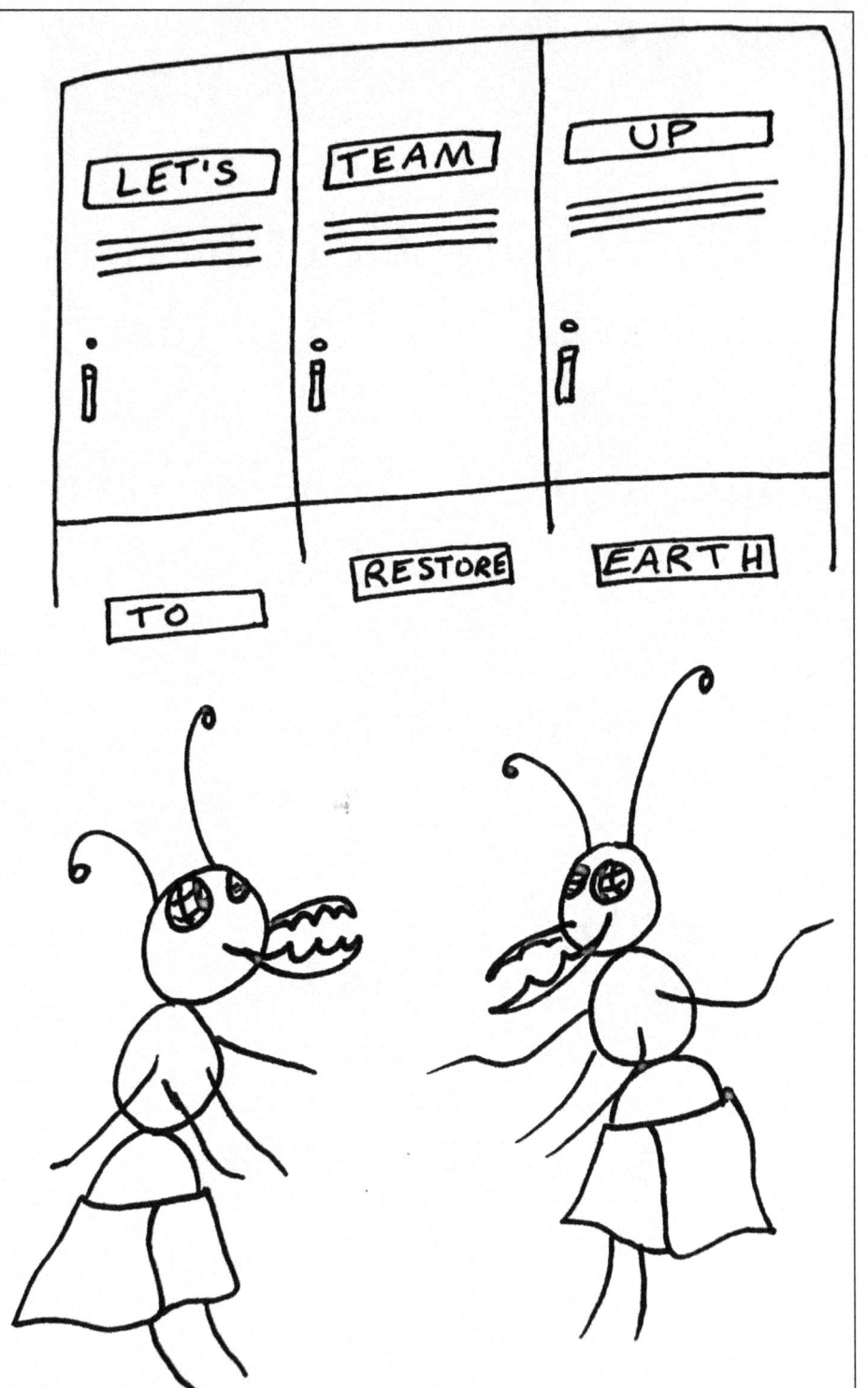

"Bro... I had some of the good stuff today... I'm flying now."

"Oh wow, Dog... You high on the Breath of Life?"

"You know it!"

"Amazing. You know, I'm drunk on Love and Joy?"

"Doesn't surprise me!"

"Bro. You played like a woman today. You were literally swimming down the court."

"Yes. Thanks for noticing- I totally felt the Great Earth Mother coursing through my veins."

"I gotta say, I'm a little jealous."

"No need Brother- she flows through all of Life- including you!"

"Thanks for the reminder."

"Dude, you scored some major points today, even when we were in a pinch."

"But did you see how kindly I responded when one of our opponents took a fall? How I helped him back up?"

"Yeah, Bro, that's what I was referring to. So compassionate. What kind of points did you think I was talking about?"

"Right? What else matters?"

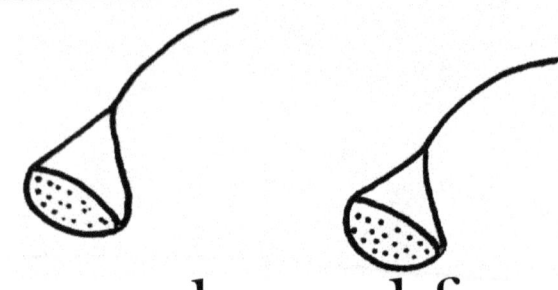

"Bro, I am so charged for today."

"With Blessings that behoove all Beings?"

"You know me too well. Pound it."

"Brother... you are such a model of inner peace. You are seriously buzzing with it."

"Look who's talking, Brother. Not to mention, your kind words are like nectar."

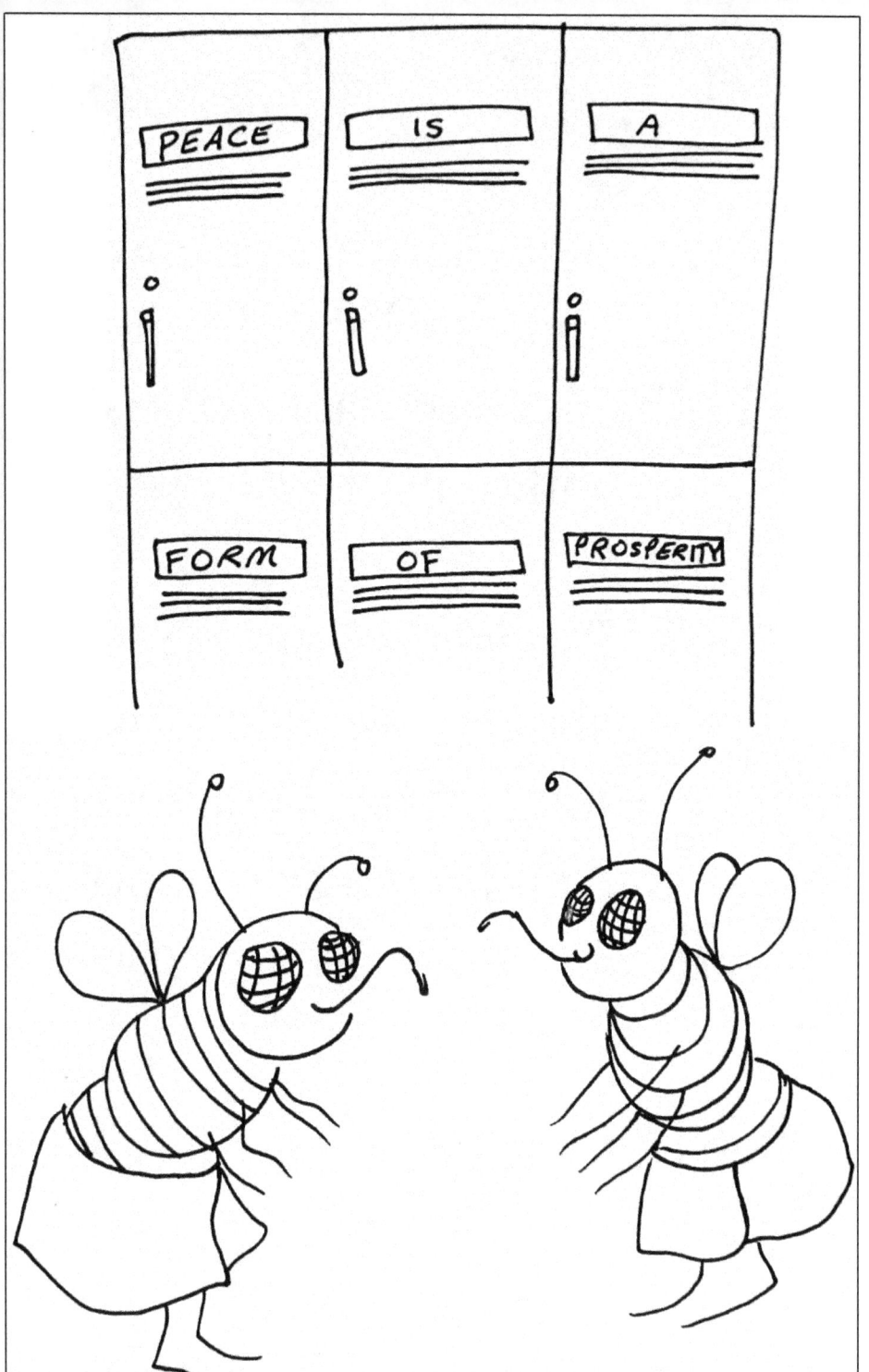

"Brother, did you see how *different* that guy looks from us? Probably thinks and roams different, too!"

"Yeah. Just when I thought we knew all the possibilities - he comes along. What a chance to celebrate and be in awe of how many ways there are to exist!"

"That's what I'm talkin' about!"

"Bro- that was so kind and respectful of you."

"Ha! I'm going to go out on a limb and share that what I did was far exceeded by the gentleness, compassion and generosity that you just revealed!"

"Whoa, Man... *Someone* is brave, secure and rooted enough with himself to express deep and authentic appreciation of others... I'll leaf it at that."

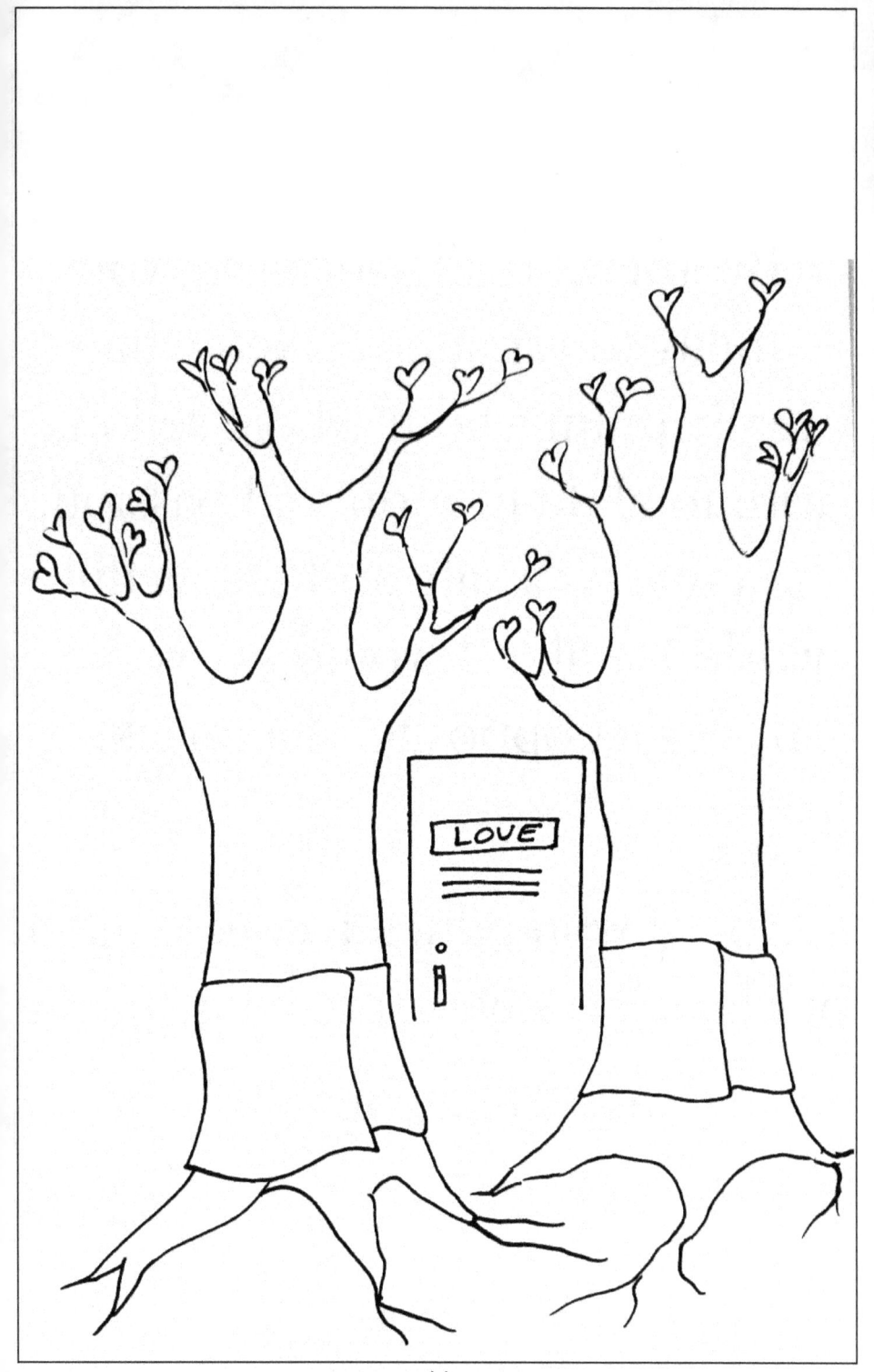

"Brother... really admiring your ability to remain relaxed while really putting your whole self in, with total dedication and passion, to creating a safe and respectful world for all... I would say you're the exact opposite of a quack."

"Bro... I won't duck a compliment but let's just say you're an inspiring individual yourself."

"My Deer Brother,
I really appreciate your uniqueness."

"Same."

"Women are sacred. All life flows from them."

"Yeah, honoring the feminine is da balm."

"Now that's a herd mentality I can buy into."

"Bro… I really appreciate how my beloved somehow always seems to provoke my insecurities so I can refine myself and clear out my personal mud."

"Totally hearing you, Brother. You are so oinking lucky to have such an opportunity to evolve."

"I really appreciate how well we focus on doing our individual and team best, simultaneously."

"That is really the best thing about being on a team with you. Being in balance together. I'm tickled pink by the opportunity to support and be supported by each other. To experience our equality."

"Bro- I need to let out a good cry. It might come out as a croak."

"Brother- how did you get to be so brave, to be so authentically sensitive to the pain of the world?"

"Part of it's having friends like you."

Any Locker Room Talk ya need to get out? Whatcha waiting for?

Call him up!

Go for a walk!

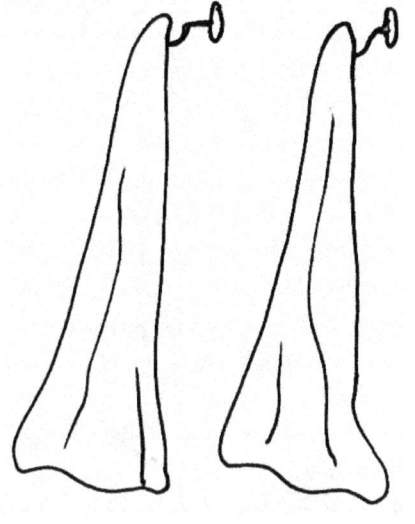

The friEnd

"Life is so precious."

"Yes. But that doesn't explain why I have to wear a towel..."

"Bro... it's because we're in the locker room."

About the Author

Oshri is thankful to create art every day. He also plays woodwind instruments and likes to plant trees and make healthy sweets. He has a bachelor's degree in Psychology from Duke University and a Master's Degree in Management from Duke's Fuqua School of Business. He is a certified mediator, dialogue facilitator and yoga instructor. You can follow his artwork on Instagram through @oshrihakak and find more of his books on ButterflyonBooks.com . Oshri really appreciates that you've taken the time to read this book and hopes it inspires you to Love.

Enormous Thanks to the following people who supported me in creating this book...
Bhumi Purohit,
Daniel Lockman,
Ezra Dror,
Hillary Barker,
Ken Borochov,
Omar Minwalla,
Patricia Clearly

Thank you to my family and friends for your love and support, and all of you who inspire me to be a better human every day.

BUTTERFLYON BOOKS

www.ButterflyonBooks.com

www.ingramcontent.com/pod-product-compliance
Lightning Source LLC
Chambersburg PA
CBHW071123030426
42336CB00013BA/2185